THE RICHEST MAN
IN BABYLON

Visit our website for more of
the greatest success guides ever written
www.SuccessBooks.net

As a Man Thinketh by James Allen
Think and Grow Rich by Napoleon Hill
The Science of Getting Rich by Wallace D. Wattles
The Way to Wealth by Benjamin Franklin
A Message to Garcia by Elbert Hubbard
The Art of War by Sun Tzu

CHARLES CONRAD

The
RICHEST
MAN *in*
BABYLON

SIX LAWS OF WEALTH

BEST SUCCESS BOOKS

PUBLISHER'S NOTE

This is an original work inspired by George S. Clason's classic parables of Babylon, which were published as pamphlets and distributed by businesses and banks during the 1920s. Writing in the antiquated style of the King James Bible, Clason used ancient Babylon as a setting to teach fundamental financial principles. In this book, financial educator Charles Conrad tells the tale anew, imparting these vital lessons in contemporary language for today's readers.

CONTENTS

FOREWORD

A T the dawn of civilization, Babylon was the greatest city on earth. It rose like a shining jewel between the banks of the Tigris and Euphrates rivers, an area called the Fertile Crescent. Here, people first created a written language, a code of law, and a system of banking.

Other lands had greater natural resources, but Babylon became rich primarily through human intelligence and ingenuity. Babylon has since faded into the mists of history, but we can still learn much from the principles upon which it was built—especially the Laws of Wealth.

Today, America and most of the world is mired in a Great Recession. This book is meant for ordinary people who are struggling to get by in these tough times. Through an entertaining story, it teaches the fundamentals of finance—how to save more of your income, get out of debt, make wise investments, increase your earning power, and safeguard a lasting fortune.

A nation's economy is only as healthy as the finances of the individuals within that economy. If more of us learn to apply these timeless Laws of Wealth, the economy as a whole will come bounding back.

Can a legendary tale of Babylon really help restore the modern world's financial health? Read on and see . . . for the road to the future runs through the past.

—CHARLES CONRAD

CHAPTER I

SEVEN THOUSAND years ago, there lived a man named Nasir, who was said to be the richest man in Babylon. Many people were jealous of Nasir because of his fine home, silk clothes, and many camels. It was rumored that he had obtained his gold by cheating and stealing from others.

One day, while his caravan was passing through the streets, one of his old schoolmates ran up to him. "Nasir!" he shouted. "Do you remember me?"

Nasir peered through squinted eyes. Then a smile broke across his face. "Ravi? Could it be?"

"Yes! Remember how we used to play together in these streets?"

Nasir commanded his driver to halt the camels. He leapt from his carriage and embraced his old friend. "How are you, Ravi?"

Ravi looked down and kicked at the dirt. "Not so well, my friend, not so well. My wife needs more fabric to sew clothes . . . my children need more food . . . the landlord demands payment for last month's rent. But my wallet is empty—I don't have a sheckel to my name. I work harder and faster each day at my carpentry shop, but my income disappears even faster."

Suddenly, Ravi had a flash of inspiration. "Tell me, Nasir . . . you and I were once the same." He looked his childhood friend in the eyes. "We grew up in this very neighborhood. How is it that you have grown so rich, while I have stayed poor? I don't believe the things they say about you, for I always knew you to be honest. So tell me—are you just lucky? Or am I cursed by the gods?"

Nasir laughed and put his hand on Ravi's shoulder. "It has nothing to do with the gods, or luck. It's simply that I have obeyed the Laws of Wealth, and you have not."

"*Don't follow the laws of wealth?!*" Ravi was taken aback. "Why, I follow every law in the Code of Hammurabi! I never lie, cheat, or steal."

Nasir smiled. "The laws of which I speak are not found in the Code. In fact, no one has ever written them down."

"Tell me," Ravi begged, "what are these laws? Please tell me!"

Nasir thought for a moment. He knew that rich men had always kept the Laws of Wealth as a great secret, carefully guarded. Yet he pitied his dear friend, who reminded him of his younger self. "All right, Ravi. I see that you are pure of heart and eager to learn." He gestured towards a café not far up the street. "Come—let us sit and drink, and I'll start at the beginning . . ."

How Nasir Learned the Secret

WHEN we were both children, Ravi, I looked around the city and noticed how some free men worked all day long but never accumulated any gold, as if they were slaves. Meanwhile, others lived in ease, and seemed to grow wealthier—even while they slept!

It is often said that money doesn't buy happiness, which is true—but only up to a point. As you know too well, people who must struggle each day for their food and shelter, deeply in debt, never sure how they will pay their bills and have money left for dinner—such people live in fear and anxiety.

But those few who have mastered the Laws of Wealth— they enjoy freedom, and live in peace and contentment.

You've heard stories about men who are rich yet miserable . . . Generally, it is those who come into gold suddenly, without earning it, who wind up miserable. Remember our friend Kuri? He drew the winning ticket in a lottery and won a hundred gold coins. He was overjoyed for several weeks, buying the finest silk robes and rarest wines as fast as he could hand out his coins to the merchants. Three months later, he was out of gold—and in fact *owed* the merchants for items he had purchased on credit. He was worse off than when he started!

Wealth—when earned by hard work, careful planning, and wise investment—is a great blessing. It allows you to eat the tastiest and healthiest foods, and to live in a beautiful home with fine furnishings. This benefits not just your family but many others, as you pay farmers, fishermen, carpenters, metalworkers, and artisans for their goods and services. It allows you to sail and explore distant lands. Or, you may choose to build a temple to the gods. In these ways and more, money well-spent nourishes both the body and the soul.

When I saw all this, I became determined to acquire wealth. But as the son of a humble craftsman, and not particularly clever or smart, I knew that it would take a lot of study and discipline. As a wise teacher once said, learning is not just about knowing the things you know—it also requires knowing what you *don't* know.

So the first step in my journey to wealth was realizing that I didn't know how the rich acquired and managed their money. When I reached adulthood, I worked as a scribe, carving words into clay tablets day after day. Like my father before me, I earned just enough money to keep myself clothed and fed, but never enough to pay back all my loans and avoid paying interest to my creditors.

One day, a wealthy money-lender named Arishaka came to me, urgently demanding a rush order on a long document. "I *must* have a copy of this contract by tomorrow," he said.

"But this contract will take at least ten tablets," I objected, "and each tablet is two hours' work."

"Finish the job by tomorrow and I'll pay you ten sheckels extra," he said.

This was the opportunity I'd been waiting for—I didn't need the extra coins so much as I needed his knowledge. "Arishaka, let's strike a bargain," I said. "If you tell me the secret of how you became rich, I'll make sure your tablets are ready in the morning, no matter what it takes."

"You've got a lot of gall," he chuckled. "But we'll call it a deal."

That night I carved by candlelight till my hands and back ached. Then I fired up the kiln and baked the tablets—fifteen in all—till they were hard as stone. When Arishaka returned the next morning, his contract was ready.

"You fulfilled your part of the bargain," Arishaka said, "so I will fulfill mine. I've never revealed my secret to any man, but I admire your thirst for wisdom. Most young people wouldn't even bother asking—they think that the rules of my generation no longer apply to them.

"But the Laws of Wealth are unchanging," he continued. "More solid even than than the words you've carved upon these clay tablets."

"Yes," I said, hardly able to contain myself. "But what are they?"

"You asked for my secret, and here it is . . . I found the way to wealth when I discovered that *a part of all I earned was mine to keep.*" He paused, stared into my eyes intently, then smiled and turned to leave.

"Wait!" I pleaded. "Surely you have more to tell me. I worked all night on these tablets!" I felt cheated and humiliated.

"Mark my words," Arishaka said, "and they'll make you rich. *A part of all you earn is yours to keep.*"

"That's no secret," I said. "*All* of what I earn is mine to keep!"

He laughed and shook his head. "Ah, if only that were true . . . Don't you pay the tailor for your cloak? The sandal-maker for your sandals? The farmer for your wheat? The innkeeper for your lodging?"

"Of course."

"Well, how much do you have left of last month's earnings?"

"Nothing."

"Precisely. Many others take a share of your earnings, but you have none left for yourself. You've been paying everyone *but* yourself!"

I began to see his point.

"Imagine if you saved for yourself one-tenth of every month's income," Arishaka continued. "How much would you have in your account after ten years?"

"A full year's income," I answered, proud of my quick calculation skills.

"Only if you were foolish enough to bury it in a jar, and keep it from earning interest!" he said. "For if you invest your money wisely, your money will go to work for you. Each silver coin generates a little copper, which, in turn, earns even more. In order to grow wealthy, you first must save a portion of what you earn; *then* you must put your savings to work for you, so that it will multiply."

"Ah, I hadn't thought of that . . ."

"A part of all you earn is yours to keep," he repeated. "As much as you can afford to save, but no less than a tenth. *This* is the secret that turned me from a sheep-herder into a money-lender. Great wealth, like a mighty oak, starts with a tiny seed. The first coin you save is the seed from which your wealth will grow. The sooner you plant the seed, the sooner your tree will mature. And the more you feed and water the tree, by saving and investing, the sooner you'll bask in contentment beneath it's shade.

"Do you still think I've cheated you out of a hard night's work?" he asked. "This knowledge will repay you a thousand times over if you understand and act upon it."

Act upon it I did, and the same secret that had transformed Arishaka from sheep-herder to money-lender also transformed me, in due time, from a poor scribe to a wealthy trader.

That day, Arishaka gave me a gift greater than a sack of gold—he gave me the knowledge of how to create wealth. And now, dear Ravi, I entrust this same knowledge to you.

THE FIRST LAW OF WEALTH
Keep a part of all you earn.
Save at least 10% of your income.

THE SECOND LAW OF WEALTH
Put your savings to work for you.
Invest it so that it will multiply.

CHAPTER II

"THANK YOU, my friend," said Ravi. "The Law is so simple, and yet so wise . . . I pledge that from this day forth, I'll save one-tenth of my earnings.

"But wait—" The hope faded from Ravi's eyes, and fear took its place. "I almost forgot . . . first I must pay back my debts. I can't save *any* of my earnings as long as the creditors are pounding on my door, demanding the money I owe them."

"I was in the very same position," said Nasir. "But I dared not ignore the First Law of Wealth. I knew that if I didn't plant a seed by saving a tenth of my income starting that very day, I might be a very old man before my savings began to take root. And so, I devised a plan . . ."

Nasir's Plan for Conquering Debt

FIRST, I resolved not to take on any additional debt. Gone were the days of borrowing today to enjoy things that I would have to pay for—plus interest—tomorrow.

Second, instead of spending all of my income each month on food, clothing, housing, entertainment, and so on, I resolved to spend no more than seven-tenths of my earnings. I would save and invest one-tenth, in accordance with the First Law. And the remaining two-tenths would go towards paying down my debts.

I went to my creditors and explained that I would no longer run from them and avoid paying my debts. If they were patient, and refrained from raising the interest rate or charging a penalty, I would pay them a small but consistent amount each month until the debt was paid in full. The creditors, happy to get a steady payment each month rather than chasing after me, readily agreed.

Meanwhile, I faithfully saved a tenth of my income, entrusting it with Arishaka the money-lender in return for interest. For each silver coin I deposited into my account, every month I received a copper coin in return. And because I kept the coppers in my account rather than withdrawing them, they too began to earn interest.

Following this plan, I was able to pay off all my debts by the year's end. At the same time, I had planted the seed of my life's fortune. Moreover, by paying back my creditors without fail, I earned a good reputation around Babylon as an honest and reliable person to do business with.

It was painful at first to reign in my spending and cut out all extravagances. But any pain was far outweighed by the pleasure of sleeping easy at night, knowing that soon I would be a free man.

For true wealth is freedom, while debt is slavery. No matter how rich a man appears—if he rides in a bronze chariot and wears fine robes—if he has purchased such luxuries on credit, he is ultimately a slave to his creditors.

THE THIRD LAW OF WEALTH
Avoid debt.
The poor pay interest,
while the rich earn interest.

CHAPTER III

LISTENING to these tales of Nasir's humble beginnings, Ravi was in awe. "As soon as I return home," he said, "I will tell my wife of these Laws of Wealth. We will pay down our debts, plant the seed of savings, and—instead of borrowing to splurge on indulgences—we'll soon enjoy the sweet taste of freedom.

"But there must be even more that I need to know," Ravi said. "Surely no man can amass a great fortune working as a carpenter, such as myself. Didn't you quit your work as a scribe and begin trading jewels?"

Nasir laughed. "That I did, and it was a huge mistake! Let me tell you the whole story . . ."

Nasir's First Foray into Investing

A year after learning of the First and Second Laws of Wealth, with a small but growing savings, I began seeking new opportunities to invest my money for a fast profit.

One day, Balashi the brick-maker came into my shop with a proposition. He told me that his cousin was about to set sail for Tyre, to purchase rare jewels from the Phoenicians. Back in Babylon, these jewels would easily sell for twice the original price. As a friend of Balashi's, I had a "golden opportunity" to get in on this scheme.

And so, I had Arishaka return all of the savings I had entrusted to him, and I gave it to Balashi.

"Are you sure this is a wise investment?" Arishaka asked. I told him it was, for in a matter of weeks I was certain to double my money.

The next month, Balashi's cousin triumphantly returned from Tyre. But the triumph was not to last—it turned out that the crafty Phoenicians had sold him worthless bits of glass, carved and colored to resemble gems.

When I told Arishaka what had happened, he shook his head knowingly. "I tried to warn you, but knew that you had to learn by experience. Only such a painful loss can cure a man of the fever for speculation."

"How can I learn to tell a wise investment from a foolish one?" I asked.

"Find a solid, established business that you understand," he said. "One that consistently makes a profit and returns dividends to its investors. If you're interested in a business you don't yet understand, find someone who does.

"If you want to learn about jewels, for instance, apprentice yourself to a jeweler. What does a brick-maker know about jewels? Nothing! But he could tell you a lot about bricks, which would be valuable if you want to become a landlord, investing in homes and other buildings for rent."

"I'm only a scribe," I mumbled. "All I know is clay tablets."

"Nonsense!" he interjected. "You're skilled in language and communication, which puts you far ahead of most. And remember this—the best investment you can make is in yourself. Continue to educate yourself and seek out wisdom, adding new skills and experiences that will make you more valuable.

"Don't be discouraged," Arishaka added. "Your savings is gone, but with the knowledge you've gained, you'll replenish it much faster than it took the first time around. The more you practice the Laws of Wealth, the more you'll attract gold like a magnet."

He was right. A year later, I befriended Ubar, the bronze-worker. Each spring, Ubar would import a large shipment of bronze from overseas, which he would spend the rest of the year molding and hammering into shields, helmets, breastplates, and swords. His craftsmanship was superb and his work in high demand; but he was having trouble paying up-front for such a large shipment of bronze. And so, understanding his business and seeing that it was reliable, I invested part of my savings to help him pay for his bronze. After several months, he returned my investment along with a hefty profit.

This was my first entry into the metal trade, and as time went on I continued to invest—not only by helping to purchase Ubar's bronze, but by adding to my own store-house of knowledge, skills, and experience.

By losing all of my savings to Balashi's cousin, I learned to diversify my investments. Never again would I give all my money to one person, or put it all in one place.

THE FOURTH LAW OF WEALTH
Don't speculate in get-rich-quick schemes.
Invest in solid businesses that you understand.

THE FIFTH LAW OF WEALTH
Invest in yourself.
Gain knowledge and skills
to increase your earning power.

As my fortune grew, I also purchased insurance policies to protect my possessions against theft and calamity, and to insure an income for my family if I were to be taken from this life.

Just as Babylon has endured countless attacks because of the great walls surrounding her, you must take precautionary measures to safeguard your growing wealth.

THE SIXTH LAW OF WEALTH
*Safeguard your growing fortune
with diversification and insurance.*

CHAPTER IV

Ravi was so caught up in his friend's story, he didn't even notice the sun sinking behind the hills. Nasir shook the last drop of wine from the bottle, then sank back on the café couch. He, too, had relished this time with a childhood friend, telling his tale and imparting the wisdom he'd learned along the way.

"If only Babylon were full of men like you, Ravi," Nasir reflected. "Honorable and eager to practice the Laws of Wealth. Most of the people live as though they had holes in their pockets. No sooner do they earn a few coins for their week's labors, than the coins fall back into the hands of the money-lenders. The bankers grow richer by the hour, while the poor lose even what little they have.

"Though I'm among the rich, I don't wish to profit at anyone else's expense," he reflected. "After all, the city of

Babylon can be no healthier than the people living within its walls. A strong Babylon depends on a strong, independent citizenry. If all citizens followed the Laws of Wealth, more money would be saved and invested, more homes would be built and adorned, more goods would be bought and sold—merchants, tradesmen, herders, builders, bankers—all would profit together."

"I'll do my best to teach others about the Laws of Wealth," Ravi said, "beginning tomorrow, with my own family. Perhaps if I can set a good example, my life will be like the single coin from which your vast fortune grew. Today, you made an investment in me by teaching me these laws. I promise to return your investment with interest, by spreading this knowledge to others."

And so, Ravi the carpenter returned to his home, hopeful and determined. The next day, he began building a great wooden plaque, upon which he carved the Six Laws of Wealth, both as a reminder to himself and a revelation to all who were blessed to pass by his door.

The First Law of Wealth
Keep a part of all you earn.
Save at least 10% of your income.

The Second Law of Wealth
Put your savings to work for you.
Invest it so that it will multiply.

The Third Law of Wealth
Avoid debt.
The poor pay interest,
while the rich earn interest.

The Fourth Law of Wealth
Don't speculate in get-rich-quick schemes.
Invest in solid businesses that you understand.

The Fifth Law of Wealth
Invest in yourself.
Gain knowledge and skills
to increase your earning power.

The Sixth Law of Wealth
Safeguard your growing fortune
with diversification and insurance.

WWW.SUCCESSBOOKS.NET

Visit us online for free books and more!

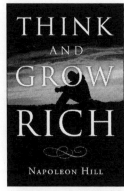

Think and Grow Rich
by Napoleon Hill

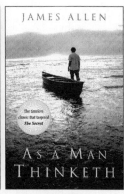

As a Man Thinketh
by James Allen

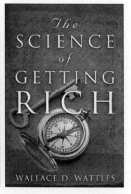

The Science of Getting Rich
by Wallace D. Wattles

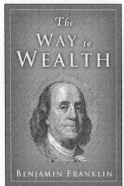

The Way to Wealth
by Benjamin Franklin

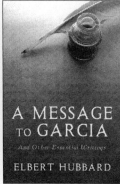

A Message to Garcia
by Elbert Hubbard

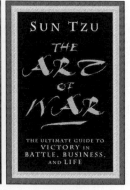

The Art of War
by Sun Tzu

Made in United States
Troutdale, OR
10/09/2023

13544572R10022